XIPHOID PROCESS

Also by Kevin Connolly

Asphalt Cigar
Happyland
Drift
Revolver

XIPHOID PROCESS

POEMS

KEVIN CONNOLLY

ANANSI

21 20 19 18 17   1 2 3 4 5

Library and Archives Canada Cataloguing in Publication

Connolly, Kevin, author
Xiphoid process / Kevin Connolly.
Poems.
Issued in print and electronic formats.
ISBN 978-1-4870-0199-5 (hardback).—
ISBN 978-1-4870-0186-5 (paperback).—ISBN 978-1-4870-0187-2 (html)
I. Title.
PS8555.O554X57 2016   C811'.54   C2016-901541-6
C2016-901542-4

Library of Congress Control Number: 2016958370

Book design: Alysia Shewchuk

We acknowledge for their financial support of our publishing program
the Canada Council for the Arts, the Ontario Arts Council, and the Government
of Canada through the Canada Book Fund.

Printed and bound in Canada

CONTENTS

This one is for my friends

It isn't chance if you're waiting for it
—Matthea Harvey

I

XIPHOID PROCESS

ASPHALT CIGAR

Oh the heartbreak, the mean transistor...
pavement rumbling with the dove.
Turn up the sunlight. I'm in the mood for a little philosophy.

You wear these shallow cuts like an itinerary of
minor renovations. Slim men in empty apartments.
There's a lot riding on the arrival of Bernie's tears.

The stars are little plastic cheese swords.
Everything a raised hand pointing to the beach.
No one's certain if she fell or jumped,

red curtain dropped over rolling eyes.
One green sock and one blue, pair just like them
in the drawer. I wonder if we should all calm down a little.

I'm not sure we need to know where empty is;
though I am consoled by this hole where you once tarried.
The lawyers are the worst: plastic and glaring.

Every man is a woman with a man inside her, trying to get out.
A branch, a leaf, a dead gull. Nietzsche is a horse trainer
in a Dionysian frenzy. Out of life's war lurch more

puffed up philosophers. I think of my motorcycle as
my best friend. First time you're late you're fired.
Day after day, everything the same. Villages burning.

Children screaming. Bright windows. Bright fires burning.
As a child I stole change from my mother's purse.
In my dreams, my face is an ocean.

A brick, seen from the window of a hurtling taxi, is a pure object.
Two women gather near the steps of a clocktower:
Monika says we must face our irrelevance.

Brittany says relevance is an illusion. Speed creates pure
objects, but they are objects speed does not understand.
Think of death as a heavy backdrop collapsing on the diva.

Sound, during its birth, was a finite place.
Life, and her darling oddball, the air, grow increasingly beautiful.
The phonograph shouts *dance dance dance dance to the radio*.

When I use the word *sleepless* it's too good for the room:
the swimmer, the drugstore, the painted word.
You expected all of this would stay the same, at least

in your head. In the room the fat men come and go,
talking of Ida Lupino. Hammer, two screws. Ball of string.
Small, useful things you'll keep but find no home for.

4

HAPPYLAND

I'll call you my symptom, my afternoon peach.
Drowsy boat conjuring mountains in the nimbus.
Strange instrument: motorless and unassembled.

At least it isn't dark just yet: patterns, moray, edge.
A pause stops being a pause, starts to define us.
What they say: new daydream, new income.

School ties: chill air piloting chill seas.
It's the astronaut's wives who truly know the moon.
But when was the last time you saw a decently painted van?

River a tree. Streams, branches. Street a short leash,
a smile at the wrong stranger. Hard work waking the dead.
Specials rotate Thursdays. Fish day's always the same.

It's midnight on the moon. Leaves turning over like
children's hands. Left fielder sleepy in the haze.
Frogmen bellow and the air suits cruise. A door opens;

a thought emerges: light-show storyboarded.
Matchstick houses, massive slumbering dogs.
Ice-heavy branches, gathering handshakes,

headed for home. Diesel, desert cedar, wet dog.
Bungalows silent as cue cards.
Those who need the manual read the manual.

Moonlight frosting a vacant planet.
Wet swingset, famished sun. Regret strolls
the jolly mausoleum, the singing ghettoes of dawn.

Curtains and petals. Their minstrel shimmy.
All that we do does not go around in circles.
Fence, street, sidewalk, threshold. Once sanity is

established, nothing left to settle but a hierarchy
of facts: join a line to join the line, creeping
forward. Nothing on the walls but Jesus.

The street signs overlook the firefighters
and the sleepers. Black trees flying by like fingers.
Not one element, but a painful confluence.

Door opening on another. This world, all flames.

DRIFT

Write what you know. Love: if you're smart you'll douse yourself
in it. The effect of things young on the suddenly aging.
There's no current pure enough—it's not light but memory

that crashes off the screen door. To quote a certain sea bream:
it's the saddest thing I ever imagined. Four years instead of forty,
eight over eighty. I dislike this pen, but can't find the one

that wrote a better summer. Not your average dong presiding
over the hazmats and the gone gone gone. But no harm in the fence,
carving everything into loose squares. You are a toy

delivered at daybreak. Shepherd logic: sticks and scowls.
Nothing unusual going on here, really. In the end we're
all bores. As though there was a cue, a truly elegant exit:

long yellow hallway with the doors sewn shut.
We stood there, panting, gathering ourselves for action.
The debacle that is silence, we stand in line for it:

the work of initiation cannot be hurried. Special
treat of seeing the air beaten out of everything.
The hiss of thin skin under a sensible suit.

It's not the height of the fall, but the cut of the prat.
Hungry as a dress caught on low branches. And always,
again, a one, a leaf, at a table, a window, listening.

I think it's the zebras I will miss the most, their generosity,
their homemade chardonnay. Wailing and sounds of grief.
Door pushed past panicking hinges. This? This is my

Dead by Dawn look. What do you think? Some petal
blown from Paris. The old look, minus the usual pity.
The audience is everywhere, birds bloomed in the eaves.

The thing about pain is it's poetic: sad grammar of full and empty.
A blind throng emerges: teen lovers dodging curfew. Watching life
run over the gravestones of thought. I've stopped thinking about

the sea of thought, that particular grey light (you know the one).
What grows wanes, what grows in waning, drowsy feather drafting
the maelstrom. The hooks that groan in everything you touch.

Knife on the counter. Shoes stacked neatly on the squad car.
The ironic counterpoise, dance of all and nothing. I knock my head
against the gargoyle, put my tongue it its ear. But it's a cheap

business blaming the victim, well of ropes, well of reason...
fix of meaning... fingers fish-hooked by a briar of stars.
What do you care if I spill open recklessly? For *hear* read *heart*,

threat, *thread*, *dearth*, and so on. It's all good because it's all
decided, everything's a gesture, a treatise on moving forward.
Rain vanishing before it hits the ground. So drop your dark suit

carefully. Snowflake racing toward the Great Divide. Thinking
can kill you dead. Though it may never, and surely hasn't yet.
If you'd please just take your seats in the clearing, we're ready

to begin. We reach for it. It moves. We collect ourselves.
Vorticist's dream of a cold charismatic nada. None of us
will ever amount to anything—think of a hump in the middle

of the desert, with no riddles. Loser propping up loser, four
corners, four traffic lights. Nothing to see here but embers.
New rooms thundering over the same stricken tenant.

TAUTOLOGY

Back in the old days, the
middle centuries, I think
you called them in Bulimia,
I was writing the same poem
you were writing just now
while deciding if that funny
smell on the bacon was something
it picked up from something else
in the fridge or whether I'd be safer
just to throw the whole package out.

And it was just then, as you were
pondering the terribly important
title assigned to this new creation—
"The Fragile Ship of Want Storms
the Blind Corridors of Devon,"
"When Wonder Flies," or perhaps
something more elegant, like,
"Tautology of Dusk"—you realized
I'd written *middle centuries* when
you'd meant *middle age* or *Middle Ages*,
Bulgaria when I'd meant to write
bulimia, or its exact opposite,
which, when you think about it,
is never exact at all.

To top it off, I admit you're going
to have to look up *tautology*
for me anyway. Though you're
obliged to leave it in here at the end,
(I know) for accuracy's sake.

WERE HE HERE

There are sentries in the sea beans,
gnats running the government.
The spring leaves, their annoying hustle,
hushed gossip in summer branches....
What is there and always was, then never is
yet is ever-present, watches over feather and
wing, plumbs puddles of air.

What evades and later proves convincing.
What convinces yet tilts its eye in a lie.
Wink at the cat and it winks right back.
But does it mean to? Or is it just verifying:
I am here, you are, we need to start with
at least that much or why start at all?

The murmur in the basement, tap
at the pane—is it always invention?
Absence of the forest, then its roaring
presence. Fish under the river, birds over.
Insects rowing it; the day's blue face.
We are lost as they are found.

A train flies into the night,
rumbles at our hands.
Machine singing through the iron bones.
Train that pushed west to greatness,
same train that crushed my penny's face

flat, then bulleting into the green.
Everything the mirror, not the glass but its
sly echo; promise of permanent
now, then a farewell frost of breath.

True, we see things in it—they're there,
we think, or we feel them around us, still
always over or behind, always stopped
mid-stride, Bigfoot-blurry, behind the known

body's ticking places; shadow carved,
then the knot pulled straight,
an owl's empty stare, slow emergence
of prey, always too timid and too many.

That ever-running film of childhood:
skittish weather, blue-eyed feathers of peacocks.
A previousness always passing, pooled blood
blushed under skin, then spirited away.

HIPSTER ON A FIXIE

Hipster, the simplicity of your one-gear ride is an apt
metaphor for what mostly goes on between your ears.
Your 100-mile vegan diet might make sense if you
could cook. It's not the fact you're thin that grates, it's how.
Hipster, I agree that Louis C.K. is hilarious, and DFW was cool.
But isn't that like saying Niels Bohr was clever, pho is delicious,
or the National has put out four straight great records?
What I don't know is a vast and growing sea, Hipster,
and you're providing exactly zero help with that.
Hipster, it's not that your no-brakes hop over four lines of streetcar
tracks in the wrong lane in Chinatown was completely insane.
It's that I wanted you to fall and I'm normally a caring person.
It's not that you're unemployed, it's that you're unemployable,
too vague to remember your shifts, too weak to lift a thing.
It's not the glasses when you don't have a prescription.
It's not even the wallet chain. Not really. It's that the wallet is
somehow always full, and leather when you're all "meat is murder."
Hipster, I don't blame you for those trucker hats or your suede
sport coat with the faux-fur collar you found at Courage My Love.
But when you're lined up at the bar sloshing draft Blue Ribbon
through those spotty beards you look like a casting call for *Das Boot*
and I loved that movie up till now. You're white as a rabbit, shaky
as a colt, but Hipster, I don't hate you because you're young,
I hate you because you're you. But you're not all bad.
You make Kensington Market in 2016 look much like
Kensington Market in 1993. You'd love your pet,
if you could look after one. You buy local, think green,
and are totally going to remember to vote next time.

"Hate is a powerful emotion," Rita said to Glenn in *Gilda*,
but you have no idea who I'm talking about, do you Hipster?
That too makes me hate you so much I fear I'll die of it.
Hipster, I know. If we met in person you'd see I'm not that angry,
and I'd probably admit you're not quite the tool I take you for.
So let's join hands, Hipster. Let us arise and go to Innisfree. Or maybe
just to Longo's to get you something to put in the fridge.
We'll have a drink at 3 Speed, another at the Dakota.
I'll tell you about my cycling dreams. You'll throw the I Ching.
Then we'll pedal out into the green mess of June as brothers.

AUTUMNAL

Keep your dance of all and nothing, slapstick trumps everything.
Fish fly in water, water turns the river's spine.
Swallows paint a November sky with the knives of their wings.
Fired moon roars awake, crashes off the cityscape.
A child kneels astride her brother's face and farts.

It's not the height of the fall but the cut of the prat.
Tramps like us and we like tramps. Not my line but what else is new.
Arms akimbo, fingers splayed. Semaphore or Noh gesture for oak?
There's nothing worse than being told something you already know. Unless it's
being told something you know in a way less complex than you already know it.

Gizmo Williams vs Pinball Clemons. Who would win?
Sontag died screaming. Keats wept every morning he awoke still alive.
And yet here they are, paper boats adrift on a sea of thought.
Some are born to greatness; others have born-ness thrust upon us.
And death shall have no dominion. Blah blah blah fucking blah.

Manic clarity often precedes a plunge into madness.
Smile. Keep moving. Keep moving and don't ever stop.

XIPHOID PROCESS

To hell with equanimity, I fucking hated turning fifty.
Longevity, morphology, incept dates. Not much I've done could be called
questionable and only acrobats or stuntmen switch horses mid-race.
Elizabethan jockeys had it rough. Not just the outfits, but all those
awkward sidesaddle races. I'm not even sure I'm making that up.
Do you think they ever call single women "fillies" in Philadelphia?
Female horses, even? It's something else; I'd stake my cheese on it.
But thoroughbreds are for royal birthdays, the coffee is for closers,
and hard drugs are for the bartenders and the bartenders' friends.
There's no Coast of Nebraska, but I've seen a small tide of snow geese
wash up over an I-80 overpass near Ogallala with my own eyes.
Joseph Conrad made more eye contact than anyone in human history.
Said people's personalities leapt out at him "like tigers."
How then to explain that last confused third of *Heart of Darkness*?
Tough to think about ending when you've just begun to begin, so to speak.
Still the "dirt nap" crowds, morphs into a game changer;
a bit like finding out odour, any odour, is particulate. Let that
settle for a minute while I fix us another mockingbird.
You want to be Sherman then language must be Old Atlanta:
taken by force. Burn it all down, don't leave a single breathing word.
Can't take a walk now after a rain without someone yelling,
"cliché!" and cliché has always been my Appomattox.
The Anasazi were either aliens or a rogue tribe of the Hopi. It's also
possible they never existed, much like Jesus, John Lennon, and Pete Rose.
Destiny's Child is yesterday's news, but someone's busy making Oreo portraits.
The further west you get, the more the traffic sounds like donkeys.
Appendix, hamate bone, xiphoid process; did they really lose their
sense of purpose, or could it be they just never found one?

A lake changes colour with the weather. Clouds are unreliable.
That tree is very far away; so far, it's almost not worth mentioning.
Cheyenne went into battle mounted backwards, Scots rode bagpipes;
perhaps the only two known examples of military sarcasm.
The Tuareg are the handsomest of desert peoples. Or maybe they just
know better photographers. Such things shouldn't keep you up nights sweating.
But was any of it ever important? Or is it more like mixing up your
jetsam and flotsam, those weeks you spent thinking Paul Douglas
was William Bendix when of course he was always Paul Douglas.
What lives over bone is fragile, doomed, really—I'm repeating myself,
but what else is there to do? You weren't listening the first time.
Wail, whelp, mate, replace yourself with a smaller you. What's that take?
Twenty-five, thirty years if you take a few pitches. So what about the rest,
now the "gone-tomorrow" pub crawl hasn't played out as expected?
Forty years is too long to perfect a romesco sauce. Just ten thousand
hours makes anyone an expert at anything, including expertise.
Virtuosity, surprise, emotional risk. Okay. But where'd my work ethic go?
A serial philanderer once told me never tell a woman she looks
great in something. "Say instead, 'That dress looks great on *you*.'"
I have nothing good to say about the man, but he never spent a
Friday night alone and only a poet could find the sadness in that.
"The future starts now," says Steve McQueen, who did all his own driving.
Nothing to be done, every day above ground, yadda yadda.
It's peaks-only from this point forward; we'll run roughshod over the interstices.
Tip of the iceberg, some call it, but what they never tell you is
the tip is always (always?), well at least almost always the best part.

REVOLVER

We're used to a season progressing logically, winter to spring.
Pick up the pace babe, we're not paying you to look pretty.
There really are people who think about this all the time.

It's all sounding very much like me all of a sudden:
the one tired gesture, awning troubled by rain;
future arced overhead like a flashlight on a child's bedsheet.

Let us be thankful for the fools: naked people and so on.
Given space, even shadows rejoice, conjoin, conjure.
In a way too complicated to acknowledge

all footage mimes the flight patterns of bees.
Grammar is green; lovely is red.
The girl who attended Carver lives next door.

Melodrama. Diphthong. Dandruff. Rhizome.
Interpretation: that's where the problems start.
Can you think of a more apt metaphor for our distress?

An understanding: that we must never tell the truth.
Shadow on the bed humming; as if this sense of being
grounded, this sudden quiet... and yes. Yes... of course it was.

Let's decide now it's all a euphemism: from those
who ducked to those who ran a quiet camera over it.
The sun was good-natured most of the time.

Pictures in which she looks happy though the journalist is sad.
What lives over bone is fragile. Doomed, really.
Tiny acrobat walking a rope of milk.

Having served up so many slices of yourself over the
years...the little hands shoved up under your jumper;
in deep grass, light panting under a yellow umbrella.

Ditties for the dead, speaking parts. Your figure less than
Greek, a little weak. All night some nights. Most, I'd guess.
Skipping classes, warnings, footprints on the bread.

The sound of rain annihilating itself on the grass.
These skies unchanging, irreversible, inexcusable,
push you out onto the porch in hope or worry.

How could something so rote find time to surprise?
The art of sounding colours as they stray. Being what
they are, photos capture the watcher's tones.

Like goats or flowers, like reeds, even swimmers gawk at
stones in rivers. But is it so wrong to want? So terrible
to love the rain? Beautiful as it always is.

II
SONG

SONG

after Walt Whitman

1

Every atom observing summer grass. Cease, not

begin: never good nor bad. Speak at every hazard.

2

Words are shelves, crowded. I know it but shall not let it.

My mouth. I am in love with it. Listen. Filter.

3

I do not talk of the end.

Always the urge, urge of the word.

4

The effect upon me or the city I live in:

doubtful news, fitful events.

5

Only the lull I like, the hum of morning
gently plunged, tongue to heart, heap'd stones.

6

The flag of my handkerchief—hieroglyphic, colourless.
To die is different from what anyone supposed.

7

No earth, nor mate, stale or discarded,
I can't see through, cannot be shaken awake.

8

The little one sleeps in its pistol.

9

This big door, clear light, play...intertinged.
I'm here; I help. I seize the clover.

10

A safe spot to pass the night. Eyes tuck'd; bride, red girl.
She had long eyelashes, brought water, fill'd a tub.

11

Which of the young men does she like best?
The homeliest of them is beautiful to her.

12

The butcher-boy puts off his great heat in the fire.
Overhand hammers swing, overhand, so slow...

13

The negro falls on the black of moving. Niches aside,
I believe in red, yellow, violet; woods, the gamut.

14

Taste the ocean week in week out. What's nearest, easiest, is me.
Adorning myself, not asking; scattering it forever.

15

The malform'd quadroon girl, paving-man, prostitute
watching the dead sleep; these tend inward to me and

16

I am of old stuff, I course with lakes, bays. Learner, prisoner,
fancy-man: moth and dark suns. Palpably impalpable.

17

These thoughts (never yours) are nothing, or next to
nothing in the common air that bathes the globe.

18

Battles lost in the same spirit in which they are won.
To those who sank: numberless unknown...

19

this meal, touch of my lips to yours, murmur:
I might not tell everybody, but I tell you.

20

What is a man anyhow? What am I?
Whimpering, analyzed to a hair. Never apologize.

21

They arrive growing, half-held by night: large few
stars! Nodding, slumbering in liquid cloud.

22

I undress, drowse—influx, efflux—this minute that comes
to me. The wonder is always (always) how there can be.

23

It alone rounds and completes all;
baffling wonder alone completes all.

24

I do not press my fingers across my mouth.
This mix'd tussled hay of head, face I have kiss'd

25

in gloom, protected by frost. How quick a waiting
sunrise kills me: plenum of proof and everything else.

26

Death sentence: I hear its chorus. It suits me.
Cut by bitter, angry hail.

27

To be, in any form. What is that? Do I stir or merely
press? To touch is as much as I can stand.

28

Is this, then, a touch? Or am I given up by traitors?
I talk wildly, lose my wits.

29

Rain. Parting payment of perpetual loan.
Sprouts accumulate, take, stand by

30

the damp of night. Soggy clods, lover and lamp,
summits and flowered branch: all shall delight us.

31

In vain the snake sails north to Labrador.
I follow quickly, ascend to a nest in the cliff.

32

Not one is respectable or gigantic.

33

Over growing scallop'd scum and long-leaved corn.
Over the blue-flower flax, a cataract falling...

34

Some fell at once, living and dead together. Some made
a mad helpless rush. At eleven o'clock began the burning.

35

It is generally thought we are sinking.
The serene stand in beams of a moon, but they surrender us.

36

Black, impassive litter of stars overhead. Hiss of
fields by the shore—short, wild, then tapering away.

37

Keepers of morning, barred at night. Sweat sinews,
everyone retreating. I protect my hat, shit shamefaced, beg.

38

I remember now: swift blossoms worn on our sleeves.
Enough! Come forward. Continue with your questions.

39

Look under your boots. I am untranslatable. Failing to fetch me,
I'll stop (somewhere) waiting for you, waiting for me.

40

Sunshine, you light the depths only. After all that pining,
you do nothing and are nothing. I buoy you up.

41

I outbid the birds, shadows, hair on my limbs.
Bugs and dirt. This day getting ready for me.

42

The performer launches, duplicates the weakest
thought: houses, dishes, that sky up there.

43

I've known the sea of doubt. Despair and unbelief.
The past is the push of you, of me, and cannot fail.

44

It's time. I keep no huge account with its lethargic mist.
Slow strata piled in their mouths. On this spot I stand:

45

calling my name, dark. From the rocks, chirping.
Hush, there can be no stoppage. Never can be.

46

I have a rain-proof coat, left hand hooking you
round the waist: a dazzle in any timid sea.

47

I teach straying: from words, oars, shutter'd rooms.
A driver minds the needle, the moment when they are.

48

The pocketless pick cool the composed object, yet see
nothing of a face in a glass, or even the street.

49

Death, toss day with dusk: your clutch of white rose grows.
Toss the gibberish of limbs, yet stay steady and central.

50

There is that in me. It swings on more than the earth.
Brothers and sisters, do you see? It is not chaos.

51

And listener, what have you to confide? I am, but only in
the minute I contain. And who walks over me? Multitudes.

52

Lawless as snowflakes,
words descend in new forms.

III

WEATHER SHOWROOM

TWELVE OR ELEVEN

hey, I want to tell you something, okay
and I want to leave a message for you right now
because again it's ten-thirty here in New York

on a Wednesday, and once again I've made
an ass of myself trying to get to a phone
to call you at a specific time and

when the time comes for me to make the phone call
I stop whatever I'm doing, and I go and I make that phone call
at eleven o'clock in the morning in New York

if you don't pick up the phone,
at ten o'clock at night, and you don't even
have that goddamn phone turned on

I want you to know something, okay
I'm tired of playing this game with you
I'm leaving this message with you to tell you

you've insulted me...you've insulted me
you don't have the brains, or the decency
as a human being...I don't give a damn

that you're twelve years old or eleven years old
or that you're a child or that your mother's
a thoughtless pain in the ass who doesn't care

about what you do as far as I'm concerned
you have humiliated me for the last time with
this phone and when I come out there

next week I'm going to fly out there for the day
just to straighten you out on this issue
I'm going to let you know just how disappointed

I am and how angry I am with you that you've
done this to me again. You've made me feel like shit
and you've made me feel like a fool over and over

and over again and this crap you pull on me
with this goddamn phone situation
you would never dream of doing to your mother

and you do it to me constantly and over and over again
I am going to get on a plane or I'm going to come out there
for the day and I'm going to straighten your ass out

when I see you, you understand me
I'm going to really make sure you get it then
I'm going to get on a plane and turn around

and come home, so you better be ready Friday the 20th
to meet with me so I can let you know just how I feel
about what a rude little pig you really are

you're a rude thoughtless little pig, okay?

40

UNFAMILIAR

1)
I have been in the news recently
about being in a hotel naked

and I have paparazzi outside my window
and I was told by law enforcement
that if I did to call 911

Yeah...these guys are sitting in a car outside my house right now
I would like to tell the officer to have them leave
because the cops have told me to call 911
if they're outside my house

My name is Erin. My last name is Andrews.
I'm all over the news right now...
I'm the girl who was videotaped without her knowing
without her clothes on in the hotel
And I got two assholes sitting outside my house

I am too, thank you.
They're in a white RAV4
I'm in a gated community

and I don't know how they got in
Mom, can you see a license plate?
Okay, the handicapped license plate they have...
what's the license plate number?

We're trying to see...
do you see it Mom ?
I'm going to try to go to another room
and see if I can read it

I cannot believe these jerks are
knocking on my door...such *assholes*....
Mom, you're totally being obvious

What?

They're both white males...I think it's that
they know I'm here 'cause I have a car out front
so they know I'm inside

I have private security that I'm working with
but they're not with me currently
and they say call 911

okay, here's the license plate:
it's a handicapped license plate for Georgia
They're looking at me through my window...
we need to make sure we get that license plate of that car

Yeah...I'm just...I did nothing wrong
and I'm being treated like fucking
Britney Spears and it sucks...I'm sorry

Thanks. Do you know how far they are out?
Okay, Thanks

2)

911: what's the address of your emergency?
Do you want to meet with an officer?

Do you want to meet with an officer ma'am when they come out?

Ma'am what's your name?

I'm not familiar…why are you all over the news?
Really?

I'm so sorry
We'll send someone out
What kind of vehicle are they in?

What's the tag number?

Are they black white or Hispanic?
Are they black white or Hispanic?

Are you okay?

Okay the first available unit will see you as soon as possible

Oh no they should be appearing

They'll be appearing as soon as possible

MESSAGE

Hello

it's about twelve...forty-five
in the evening

my name is Judd Nelson
I play the role of Jack Jones in the movie

I have not received a call sheet
I have not received a message telling me when my call time is

I want to let you know
my name is Judd Nelson
I'm playing the role of Jack Jones
in this project

I have not received a call time
or anything

or anything under my door
or even a phone message that's blinking
on my phone here in the room
I've tried my *best*
you haven't let me know when my call time is

I'm putting a do not disturb on my phone
'cause I'm going to go to bed

what can I tell you?
what can *you* tell me?

you obviously don't care
when I come in to work tomorrow
right?
you don't
care
when
I come in to work tomorrow

I tried
I'm waiting as late as I can stay up
I've got to go to bed
I've got to work tomorrow...
who knows when?

good night

please...don't
try and reach me.

SO MUCH

I'm not someone
to go to
someone
who's the only person

that they're there for

I love you, too

so much

I'm just
confused
I'm like, caring more
than the other side

and then Mommy says
I'm like
you were
and she's defending...

and so
she says to me on the phone
like, she doesn't
back me
and she doesn't
stand by me

why?
why?

I'm fine

no one cares
about me and you
by the way

no one cares that much

it's about
how they feel
not about how
I feel

no
it's not about
me

never
gonna
be about me

unless I fight for it

BLACK COW

1

TOMALES: At 2:08 a.m. a resident on crutches reported that people had twice driven down the driveway, spinning around and throwing rocks onto parked cars.

TOMALES: At 8:48 a.m. a vehicle had slid into a "mountain."

WOODACRE: At 10:01 a.m. a woman reported the theft of copper rails.

NICASIO: At 10:37 a.m. about 20 cyclists were holding up traffic.

POINT REYES STATION: At 11:08 a.m. a teenager reported hitting a car on his bicycle by mistake.

HICKS VALLEY: At 12:14 p.m. a passerby reported an empty red Chevy sitting in the middle of the road with its flashers on.

TOMALES: At 1:34 p.m. a woman who earlier complained about vehicles on her driveway said a party was planned in the neighborhood that night. She hoped deputies would be there to quell mischief.

STINSON BEACH: At 2:23 p.m. a parked car was sticking out onto Panoramic.

STINSON BEACH: At 3:27 p.m. someone saw kids with guns on the beach. Deputies found youths with drugs, alcohol and at least one BB gun.

SAMUEL P. TAYLOR: At 5:17 p.m. two black cows were in the road.

NICASIO: At 7:37 p.m. someone saw a cow.

CHILENO VALLEY: At 6:20 p.m. a man said juveniles who had built a bonfire on his property the night before had damaged his vehicle. A similar gathering was planned for that night.

TOMALES: At 9:09 p.m. firemen took someone to a hospital.

BOLINAS: At 3:04 a.m. someone saw a white man in a red sweater spinning circles in a silver truck. Deputies found a man trying to get out of a ditch.

BOLINAS: At 8:54 a.m. a landlord asked for advice about a tenant who hadn't paid rent in months and appeared to have abandoned the property.

WOODACRE: At 9 a.m. a tenant reported the theft of copper pipe.

FOREST KNOLLS: At 11:34 a.m. medics took someone to a hospital.

DILLON BEACH: At 11:34 a.m. medics took someone else to a different hospital.

POINT REYES STATION: At 12:25 p.m. a container holding bicycles was broken into near the Dance Palace, the contents strewn around.

MUIR BEACH: At 2:13 p.m. a resident asked deputies to check for firework debris.

MUIR WOODS: At 4:32 p.m. a realtor asked for advice about posting signs.

SEASHORE: At 4:42 p.m. a man said his redheaded wife was driving to the lighthouse after talking about killing herself.

BOLINAS: At 10:55 p.m. a neighbor said an unstable woman's dog had been barking for half an hour. Deputies found the owner asleep.

3

DILLON BEACH: At 8:19 a.m. a trailer truck was stalled on a blind turn.

POINT REYES STATION: At 8:44 a.m. a laptop was reported stolen.

INVERNESS: At 10:17 a.m. a Seahaven homeowner reported the disappearance of tools, antique kitchen items and a comforter after people hired through Craigslist had come to work on the house. (Deputies noted that one subject was on probation.)

FOREST KNOLLS: At 10:35 a.m. a woman called to say she and her husband were separating amicably but that he had threatened to take their kids to Germany.

FOREST KNOLLS: At 11:20 a.m. a farm stand owner reported receiving an anonymous letter criticizing his high prices.

TOMALES: At 1:11 p.m. a woman who returned a call from someone claiming to be with the I.R.S. said the person asked her personal and obscene questions.

MUIR WOODS: At 2:51 p.m. a U.P.S. truck hit a fire hydrant.

BOLINAS: At 3:19 p.m. someone was having issues with a neighbor.

STINSON BEACH: At 4:53 p.m. the child of a 73-year-old man reported that the latter had threatened him or her with a knife.

OLEMA: At 5:30 p.m. a black cow was outside its pasture.

OLEMA: At 6:09 p.m. someone saw a truck pull onto park service property and two people with flashlights exit and start to load metal into the back.

FOREST KNOLLS: At 10:16 p.m. a Juarez Avenue neighbor complained about yelling squatters. Deputies found a woman who agreed to put out a campfire and go to bed. (A man had been yelling out of frustration, but had left to sleep elsewhere, they noted).

IV

ARENA ROCK

BRILLIANT DISGUISE

Touch a word and a world comes out. Fire.
Its captions, details. Fired clouds churning through a day.
Do you have any clue how many moons Saturn has?
I'll read them to you: Titan, Enceladus, Rhea, Dione, Mimas,
Iapetus, Tethys, Hyperion, Epimetheus, Janus, Phoebe, Prometheus,
Pan, Helene, Pandora, Telesto, Calypso with a "y," Anthe, Methone,

Pallene, Thrymr, Polydeuces, Kiviuq, Narvi…it goes on for ages.
Look at these insects' wings. Punctuation. Mourning cloaks.
They occupy space between our attentions, as barely risible
as anything else. Come on in. Find a chair. I abhor houseguests,
but then here you all are. We'll deal. Divide the salad,
share the steaks, sop up the blood with bread.

We're here. But only for the moment we're actually here:
this one (an example) where I tell a homeless woman
I "never carry cash." In this way we preserve ourselves.
Have mercy on the man who doubts what he's sure of.
The future, properly apprehended, is lag momentum. A first
set of lights. We are bad. We're probably something worse.

LOVE REMOVAL MACHINE

The day's a crown we'd all want to wear, yet
few silent stars survived the transition to talkies.
Johnny Weissmuller, as per his dying wish, was
counted out with three signature Tarzan yells.
The lord of bad choices made seventy-nine whereas second wife, Lupe Vélez
(Mexican Spitfire), rode out a cloud of Seconal at thirty-eight.
Many felt that was Gary Cooper's fault. Maybe it was.
In Keanu Reeves' return to the stage in Winnipeg, as Hamlet
no less, the audience broke into spontaneous laughter
on the line: "My excellent good friends."
Life's a bad writer. Ask the lead singers of
passable hair bands now working shifts as retail greeters
while Rush reigns as mid-America's mid-market monsters.
Great art demands a great audience. Frye boots and mullets,
see-through net vests and poets' blouses—you can guess
where things went awry with this particular cult.
Much like this crowned day; its worry it won't pass for normal.
Normal meaning the mean, mean meaning what it usually does.
The world drags you down. Still, there are doves, gold sounds,
bees having trouble with their direction. *Wild flower, I love*
you every hour. Isn't everything alive a kind of come-on?
Shadows of geese, gulls; the biggest, asteroids rolling
over your shoulders as you ride the August light.
Doorbell's been disabled, screen door latched, still you'd
swear each morning you were roused by knocking.
The Witnesses never ask for shit, but look at them—
the script, the outfits—they're selling something.

So many different ways of doing, maybe the only sure

thing is the best bad guitar solo in arena rock history.

Check the bootlegs: that dude never does it any better.

Common sense holds you can't doubt you're doubting.

But find me anything interesting that's not done at least that.

FOOLED AGAIN

This room is prettier than any room in the Bible.

I know this how? Because I have made love in this room.

Some days it was with myself—the most viable option.

It's not your place to judge. It's a living, breathing thing,

the room I mean. Open the windows strategically

and a pleasant cross breeze manifests itself, conditions

outside allowing, though I freely admit I have not been

outside for some time (and there you are again, judging).

Free will is treacherous as a concept. Which is freer,

the fly frantic to get out or the moth dying to get in?

Meet the new boss, same as the old boss.

The Irish are a naturally poetic people. Which is why

they have been slaves for more than two thousand years.

There are books in this room. Some of which have been

read and some of which might be here just for show.

Which makes this room more flexible than any in the Kama Sutra.

A line of ants marches through it every April,

like the camels and horses that roamed the Silk Road.

But comparatives are for weak imaginations, and for the ants, a

floor is more vast than a solar system, which we all mostly just imagine.

Hard to say how, but the Pluto fly-by is skewing everything.

Turns out Pluto is a red planet, despite its unimaginable frigidity.

And turns out this room is hotter than any mentioned in the Koran.

"I will leave this room better than I found it."

A thought from another poet I now share with you.

HALFWAY THERE

A stickup is not a cash advance any more
than a spaghetti strap is a footbridge.
You live for the fight when it's all you've got,
but how many weeks does a tip jar stay empty
before the whole concept is abandoned?
Few outcomes are more suspect
than those that appear certain.
An horizon, like any opera, surfs its curtains.
But it has nothing to say to you, personally.
It's been rather eloquent on that point in fact.
Even the bees, drunk on coneflower, know
it's a short stumble from muse to groupie.
Waves are neither ornate nor plainspoken.
You say Bon Joe-vi, I say Bon Jaw-vie.
Still, when things go deep on the dunes
it's only human to lurk the most recent footsteps.
Cue the shorebirds. Their diphthongs and
detritus—triptych hovering bluing light.
An easel never questions what it props up,
but listen close and you'd swear the sea
breeze just said, "Don't get cocky."
You've got to get in to get out.
My phantom limb is talking to me again.
He's saying he wants a fresh arrangement.
He's saying he wants a left for his right:
fingers for fingers, then fingers for feet.
But I'm too smart for that.
I know what he's looking to replace.

STOP BELIEVING

My devil had been long caged; he came out roaring.
Motor City is a different animal. Long memory.
Not like those plates in L.A., their constant shifts.
Hard rock is cliché's crash cart.
Groceries expire but the lists persist:
streetcars, people. Somewhere in the night
a baker wakes, eggs are delivered. A monk retrieves
an iron key from his robe. Sunday is the son's day,
but Mondays? Time to check the cheese.
Go ahead, hold on to that feeling,
but do so knowing most are better let go.
You see heads, heads only, just above
the dunes—hacked off or buried to the neck?
Yes...but no, more likely moored to something calmer
close to shore, measuring this straw-yellow day.
One Hundred Fifty Glorious Years of the Coast Guard:
bunting and funnel cakes and clowns. Whatever and who cares.
If you're so convinced death leads to eternal
bliss then why are you wearing a seat belt?
Swan following another swan—after which a wonder,
or another swan: Ruth, DiMaggio, Louis Armstrong, Earhart,
Gagarin, John Glenn, Gus Grissom, Neil Armstrong, Elvis,
James Brown, Aretha, Orr, Bowie, Perreault, Gretzky, Ian Curtis,
Stevie Y, another Armstrong, Datsyuk, Sade, Thom Yorke, and Prince.
Lungs emptied. Lungs refilled. Rings in a redwood,
small glove, pointing: "Here I was born. Here I died."

The news is blue. It has its way of getting to you.

Tags on an overpass. Birds kissing a shaking lake.

Whatever the wind was, surely it meant them no harm.

THAT OLD SOMETHING

Sadness might be all we knew. Happiness,
some days. The way the word *weird* looks
as weird spelled correctly as when it's not.
Or those trees with leaves instead
of needles (and what's *that* word, now?)
make such a big show of it each October,

holding their breaths, turning red before
the sudden tragic burlesque denuding.
"If there's an afterlife, no one will be
more pleasantly surprised than me."
A joke. Stray line delivered over beers.
Or was it, "No one would be more pleasantly

surprised if I woke up in the afterlife?"
What trips you up is order: skewed
perspective ruining an otherwise competent
pencil sketch of a covered bridge.
Conifers (yes!) hold fast to green, but
it's also possible they're better defended.

A train careers into the station, dragging
its cacophony of soot. We take no notice.
Then a bell rings and we all rush the doors.
It's probably sanest to refuse to reside with sense.
Find a more comfortable seat in some adjacent
room: Happiness. Sadness some days.
More than a feeling but less than a viable idea.

INTO NOTHING

Grade eight was all about Christy Pokarney. Her American-ness
and honeyed tan, how she smiled whitely at my borrowed jokes,
ignored the hockey hair, chose Mrs. Premise over Mrs. Conclusion.
She went for Steve Rotz in the end (perpetually snotty yet
way ahead sexually). I'm a bad boy, because I don't even miss her.
She's a (same line) she completely trashed my heart.
Once afoot, any game devolves into minutiae:
a pleasing or unpleasant scent above the nape,
shocked light over a soccer pitch (dusk, midsummer).
Cryptic message on a T-shirt; racism snared in a parasol;
sadist playing "Hey Jude" on pan flute beside the water taxi.
Tom Petty can barely get a song on the radio.
How does that happen, exactly? Cruise is bruised.
Taylor (like her cats) is très needy and exceedingly boring.
Leo is well-endowed but too swift on the trigger:
never has so much given so little to so many.
There's the rub—keep Verlander it's so long Fister and Porcello.
Ask the spokes on any wheel. Nothing true ever stays so.
What's verifiable is the same trap—free falling out into nothing.
The good old days may not return.
If memory is photographic,
we're all trending toward obsolete.
Better, then, to embrace the escalator.
When it's broken it's still stairs.

WITHOUT

Maybe there is a plan, slow-gathering, still fluid—
sky a sea on fire, but relax. It's nothing biblical.
It's happened recently, unnoticed, twin rainbows after
a weird rain, the Lowes parking lot turned chiaroscuro.
Kierkegaard is hilarious. The long game, the trauma,

grandiloquent doubt. How differently slower stories play out:
letters wandering like taxis, dandelions, ants wet with wings.
You arrive, dressed in greens and browns. Make your point
as if it seems worth making; loiter by the pool.
The little wet lights sudden as coins, etcetera.

Like someone turned off a projector, the sand goes dark.
Evening's green an ideal of fatigue, crescendo; tidesound
rampant, now snared in grass, now rushing the bed.
What you like is in the limo. But a beach is just a day.
You can memorize, but it's only known once.

Haven't you heard? It's a battle of words:
but should we go with favourite or only?
With. Without? It can't be helped, but
there's a lot of this about. Tonight we dined
by the pool. It likely saved our minds.

I hope you had there the same light, too.
The Martians. Sun through black locusts.
Those hovering figures from our pasts.

DON'T THINK

When a storm rolls in slow it makes no sound.
Through sneezing poplars, past the joe pye weed,
aphids foaming, mayflies riding out their exits.
The less you see a thing the more you look for it.
Squirrels spooned on a trunk's dry leeside.
You like to think you're immune to this stuff

but it's hard not to be them, given most outcomes.
Something wrong with my stars—can't figure out
where the Pleiades are. Why did the sister go to Hartford?
Why would she do that? And how could she marry that man?
Honey, don't think. You're liable to figure me out.
Poe died in a ditch. Wearing another man's clothes.

Samuel Clemens went bankrupt printing Grant's memoirs then,
in trying to pay it all back, invented stand-up comedy.
The tabloids cashed Amy Winehouse. "I've got to go
not so far as I can, but just as far as is needed.
Let somebody else say I made a fool of myself."
When a wind comes in hot it shivers fences,

like the past tense turns any stray page black.
It doesn't matter if you don't mind, but this
world's a hard place for little things. So
let the ants scheme. Cup the green moth mid-
flight with a shortstop's hands. As usual,
night knows what it's doing. Stay aware to all

exits. Bless what flesh you've seared or eaten.

Bury the beer and the fruit fly drinking it with you.

Mark sprinting clouds; now shadow, now light

rushing after. Constant push then the loud ungluing.

They prefer to remain unknown. The clouds, I mean.

That is, known briefly, and only from your perspective.

THE LIMIT

Since the rise of ethanol, monarchs are a doomed
species—no milkweed, no orange migrating wonder.
Plus that big dead hole in the Gulf where the shrimp
want to be. All alone at the end of an evening,
you realize with pained certainty it's plain
dread that's been running your life.
Float in a pool staring upwards, track locusts
through the locusts. Hang a lamp in night branches
above a sheet and see what turns up.
Mate and you might pass the trouble on. But leave
yourself a second exit. It's slow but it isn't stupid.
Every school kid knows about the Nickel Man:
what he's up to and why he can't abide the sun.
And now there's hail when you'd booked the barbecue,
that twitch in your neck that might be too much caffeine.

It's a Long Night at Wrong Beach. Felder's found his limit
and Meisner will not do the encore one more time. Ever.
"Only three more songs before I kick your ass, pal." Fine,
but good luck finding another man who can hit that note.
A throng emerges from the dunes—mostly teens off-curfew.
Repetition soothes but there's risk in that reward:
a mob does what it wants until it wants something
else and there's nothing a mob does that's clean.

The Navajo know Shiprock as the holiest of places.

Wreck of the great bird that brought the People

crashing to the earth. Still, it's fucked up now: you can

see it from the highway. Nightmare of empties and chip bags

in the ditches; tumbleweed against barbed wire;

cactus, dry pasture, then the tossed prehistoric spine.

The trouble with the trouble is it's all trouble.

A wise man once said, "Anyone can have a bad century...

and a bad first fifteen years of the next."

(It was Bob Ryan and he was talking about the Chicago Cubs.)

When mounting, strive to keep all wings and antennae pristine.

Push the pins in firmly. Minimize thoughtless damage.

The trick is not minding that it hurts.

KILLER PARTIES

Almost killed me — that collapse from autumn to ice.
Cloud patterns only an Elsinore could love.
Time to put the puppets down, someone said
to Edgar Bergen. And how'd that work out?
I remember we departed from our bodies.
Turns out Virginia really is for the lovers;
but Philly ran out of brotherly love sometime
during the Nixon administration.

Jack Ruby's car was a crime scene long
before he slipped in through the police
entrance and put Lee Harvey in a bag.
Most living things respect a cycle — its bite and
bark, phloem or skin; carapace, lemony eye.
Then there's the Ephemeroptera, born
sans mouth or anus — bright green things spent
in sparks, confettied in and out of being.

A man could spend a lifetime trying
to remember what he should not have said:
daisy in the memory of a shark. It's the policy
of reverence for age that makes the young bitter.
Maybe you're going to be the one that saves me
after all. As you are. As you were and want me to be.

Still … finitude. As a concept? That species of
dread is the burden of Homo sapiens;
and maybe a very few very smart dolphins.
All else just stops.

NOTES ON THE POEMS

This book is rife with plunder, most of it obvious, some of it less so. Mindful of an old adage about borrowing versus stealing, I feel obliged to confess to a few specific infractions:

The middle line of the fifth stanza of "Asphalt Cigar" belongs to James Tate.

The middle line of the ninth stanza of "Happyland" is from Hilton Obenzinger's *New York on Fire*.

"Song" is a redaction of Walt Whitman's "Song of Myself."

"Xiphoid Process" and most of the poems in the Arena Rock section include lines, bits, or concepts from stand-up comedy, including that of Doug Stanhope, Maria Bamford, and Mitch Hedberg.

The penultimate line of "Fooled Again" is a lyric by Joe Pernice.

The opening line of "Stop Believing" is from Robert Louis Stevenson. The last line is Darrell Gray's.

The opening line of "Love Removal Machine" is Heather Christle's (more or less). The observation of Keanu Reeves' performance in *Hamlet* comes courtesy of Elyse Friedman.

The fourth line in "Don't Think" is Suzannah Showler's, and the final couplet plays off a line/couplet I've always liked by Bill Knott. And "I've got to go not so far as I can, but just as far as is needed. Let somebody else say I made a fool of myself," is from an interview with Paul Scofield about acting.

The last five lines of "Without" are from a Michael Helm email.

"Black Cow" is for Liberty Valance. "Brilliant Disguise" is for Michael Redhill. "Killer Parties" is for Jason Anderson and Bill Reynolds. "Love Removal Machine" is for Zani Showler. "Message" is for Elyse Friedman. "Without" is for Michael Helm and Alex Rockingham. "Xiphoid Process" is for Matthew Tierney.

ACKNOWLEDGEMENTS

Some of these poems, usually in slightly different versions, have appeared (or will appear) in *Arc*, *Exile*, *Lemon Hound*, *Taddle Creek*, *Riddle Fence*, and *The Walrus*. The project that became this book was also greatly accelerated by grants from the Canada Council, the Ontario Arts Council, and awards from the K.M. Hunter Foundation and the Ontario Media Development Corporation. I remind myself how lucky I am to live in a city, province, and country that believe in art as something worth supporting.

Starting with Sarah, thanks to everyone at Anansi. Couldn't be easier. Thanks to my colleagues, students, and fellow travellers in the University of Guelph's MFA program. Apart from giving me something useful to do in the fall and winter, you've all changed the way I approach, think about, and practice my art.

This book was made better than it might have been by a few people, but primarily my editors David O'Meara and Damian Rogers. I owe you both, hugely but differently. I mean, who finds good edits in *found* text? Only poets.

Finally, I live with Gil Adamson (I know, right?), whose patience, intelligence, and generosity are constant. All poems are for you.

PHOTOGRAPH BY DAWN CONNOLLY

KEVIN CONNOLLY's previous collections include *Asphalt Cigar*, a finalist for the Gerald Lampert Award; *Drift*, winner of the Trillium Poetry Prize; and *Revolver*, a finalist for the Griffin Poetry Prize and Trillium Book Award. He teaches poetry in the MFA program at the University of Guelph and has been poetry faculty at the Banff Centre's May Writing Studio.